SNOW STORM

THE PRESS

THE SOUTH ISLAND'S BIG CHILL

THE ROGUE STORM

The Lake Coleridge area was hit by an overnight power cut after snow fell in the area.

PREVIOUS PAGE: Snow fell steadily through the night in Timaru — the Bay Hill at 3.30 am.

The great snow of 2006 stole in during the night to claim the land, moving across Canterbury in the early hours of Monday 12 June. People from Timaru to Fairlie, Geraldine to Ashburton, Methven to Christchurch, all remarked afterwards on the abrupt quietness, as heavy rain stopped pounding on the roof and drumming on the windows. Half-asleep, many thought it had just stopped raining.

While they slept, the snow set in, falling thickly and stealthily in the darkness. When dawn eventually crept over the Canterbury Plains, it revealed a dense white carpet smothering houses, farms, stock and trees. The snow was nearly one metre deep in some places, even deeper than the great fall of July 1945. It took almost all by surprise, and as its weight collapsed buildings, pinged power lines and blocked roads, the full force of the calamity began to be seen.

WEATHER WARNINGS

Sunday 11 June had been one of those days when any weather forecaster worth their salt would want to be at work. For several days, computer models had been anticipating that an area of low pressure, or depression, would develop into an intense storm system as it crossed the Tasman Sea, heading towards the top of the South Island.

As predicted, the system was now deepening rapidly and bearing down on the country, and forecasters at the MetService's National Weather Forecasting Centre in Wellington were frantically trying to keep pace with it, issuing and amending weather warnings for heavy rain and severe gales, most of them for the North Island. Pre-occupied as they were with

what was happening ahead of the system, the possibility of heavy snow in the east of the South Island — as what turned into a 'bomb low' (weather bomb) passed — was not foremost in forecasters' minds.

Sunday was a spectacularly warm day in Canterbury, as so often happens before heavy snow. Balmy north to north-westerly winds pushed the temperature as high as 17 degrees in Christchurch that afternoon under the nor' west arch. Keen weather watchers tapping their barometers during the day were not fooled, however, noticing how quickly the air pressure was dropping as the depression drew closer. At 11 pm it was still 14 degrees in the city, by which time snow was only a few hours away from falling in South Canterbury.

Graham Campion of Corwar estate, Barrhill, near Rakaia, clears his driveway.

The threat of heavy snow grew that evening, as forecasters realised they had a rogue system on their hands. At 8.30 pm they issued a warning saying up to 15 cm of snow could fall down to 300 m in South Canterbury overnight, with lighter falls to 200 m. There were no updates during the night. At 8.50 am on Monday 12 June, a bulletin warned of heavy snow to near sea level throughout the region. By that time, most Cantabrians had seen the snow on the ground and watched it fall in the diffuse, post-dawn light for more than an hour.

Before long, thousands of homes in Selwyn, Ashburton, Timaru, Mackenzie, Waimate and the Waitaki districts were without power, the lines fizzing under snow or poles pulled down by its weight. Giant insulator bolts snapped like frozen beans. And then the cold came.

For most, the snow would stay for three weeks. For some it would languish, frozen and refrozen, for more than six weeks.

The temperature had fallen rapidly in the early hours of Monday as the snow made its way north-east across the Plains. In Christchurch, the thermometer dropped from 11 degrees at midnight to 7 degrees by 3 am, with light rain slowly setting in and a change to south to south-westerly winds. An hour later it was 4 degrees with heavy rain and gusting winds, and by 5 am the temperature had fallen to 2 degrees. Heavy sleet turned to snow between 6 am and 7 am as the temperature dropped further to freezing point. A similar pattern of thermal change had taken place two or three hours earlier further south.

In its preliminary investigation of the snow storm, the National Institute of Water and Atmospheric Research (NIWA) said snow depths of 30 cm to more than one metre were recorded south of the Rakaia River. Those measurements were 'extreme', greater than the damaging August 1973 and November 1967 falls and akin to the July 1945 dump, even deeper in some places. Ashburton's 38 cm of snow was its greatest on record and Timaru's 30 cm was its heaviest since 1945.

North of the Rakaia, snow depths were spectacular in pockets but not record-breaking, ranging from less than 5 cm at the coast in Christchurch to 60–70 cm in the foothills. Inland falls were similar to 1973, but along the coastal plain north of the river and south-west of the city, the snow was deeper than in August 1992, 1973 or 1967. In Christchurch, the average fall of around 10 cm was about the same as the June 2002 event, but far less than the records of up to 30 cm of snow in 1992 and 40 cm in 1945.

At daylight on Monday 12 June it was still snowing heavily across much of Canterbury. It wasn't until later in the morning that a clearance in the weather slowly moved across the Plains. By early afternoon, snow had stopped falling in the majority of places.

For most, the snow would stay for three weeks. For some — particularly in the vast Mackenzie — it would languish, frozen and refrozen, for more than six weeks. At its worst, it would cover the greater part of the South Island, but it came to lie most heavily in the great farming land of Mid and South Canterbury.

THE DAMAGE

Electricity lines were down around Canterbury, the weight of snow and ice destroying more than 500 power poles around the region and cutting power to 35,000 households and businesses. Many people were without power for two weeks, and in South Canterbury it took a third week before power was back on for Alpine Energy's last affected customer.

The cold took over the days and the nights, prompting Civil Defence fears that without help some might freeze in their homes. None did, thanks to the almost universal use of logburners in regions where wood is relatively cheap and

OPPOSITE: Estimated maximum snow depth (cm) from the 12 June 2006 snow storm across the Canterbury region, not taking into account topography. Hollow circles indicate inferred data, while filled circles are actual observations. Provided by NIWA with kind permission from Orion New Zealand Ltd.

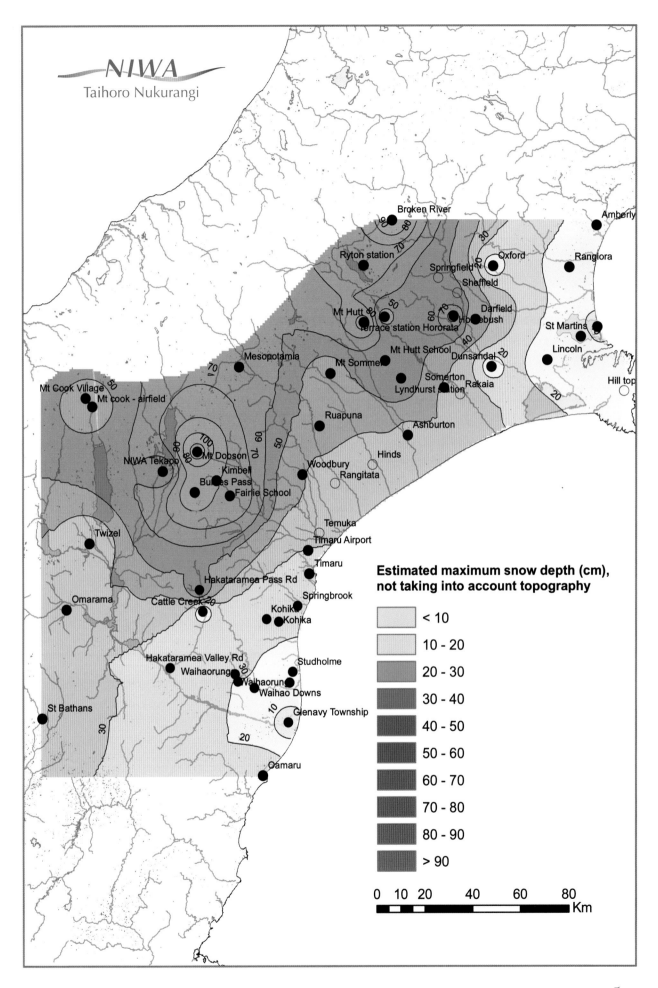

Estimated maximum snow depth (cm), not taking into account topography

	< 10
	10 - 20
	20 - 30
	30 - 40
	40 - 50
	50 - 60
	60 - 70
	70 - 80
	80 - 90
	> 90

0 10 20   40   60   80
Km

readily available. Some elderly residents, and others in homes reliant on electric heating, were evacuated. Others wrapped themselves in blankets and rode it out. Families with logburners moved in to lounges, using the burners for both heating and cooking.

In addition to the power loss, phone lines had been toppled, towns cut off, roads blocked, and schools and businesses closed.

The breakdown of telecommunications on a grand scale worsened the misery — and the danger — of the big snow. It wasn't just the lines: cellphone tower batteries went down, and so did those used to run landlines. The loss of phone links hampered attempts to assess damage, so that thousands of households were left not only without power and a way out, but also without any way to contact neighbours or authorities.

The breakdown of telecommunications on a grand scale worsened the misery — and the danger — of the big snow.

State Highway 1 was covered with 15 cm or more of snow south of Christchurch, and was closed between Ashburton and Oamaru. Also closed were parts of State Highways 6, 8 and 73, as well as Porters Pass, Arthurs Pass and Lindis Pass. Some roads on Christchurch's Port Hills were closed and hillside bus services had to be cancelled.

After three or four days, however, most major roads had been cleared by councils deploying fleets of graders, snow ploughs and front-end loaders.

While farmers were relieved the storm had arrived before calving and lambing, snow damaged shelter belts and woolsheds. Farmers out feeding stock had difficulty reaching their animals in some places because the snow was so deep.

In the Ashburton district, the emergency relief committee headed by farming veteran John Leadley swung into action. It organised helicopters to fly into remote areas to assess the stock situation. Snow-rakers went in early to get stock down to feed and — remarkably given the conditions — they brought down all movable stock within four days. The committee's swift action undoubtedly saved many lives.

Generally, stock losses were light — or as light as they can be with snow lying to great depths across the hills and plains. The great farming casualty was the early use of precious winter feed, and the toll the snow and cold took on stock condition.

Farmers, insurance agents and accountants totting up the toll of the snowstorm estimated widespread damage and farm losses would cost the economy more than $100 million. Federated Farmers believed rural Canterbury would feel the impact of the snow for at least a year and was hoping there would be no more snowfalls during the winter and spring to make sure feed reserves lasted.

There were concerns in the dairy industry that pressure on feed would affect calving and milk production when the milk flows arrived in August, with the risk of cows losing condition. Forage crops were damaged by the snow and that meant farmers were using supplementary feed at two or three times more than the usual rate.

The insurance industry said other claims from the storm were likely to exceed $35 million, most of that from collapsed roofs, broken guttering, frozen and cracked pipes, and fallen trees.

A METEOROLOGICAL MAVERICK

Forecasters admit the weather bomb bamboozled them. It was unconventional and did not progress as that kind of system does most of the time. They say that snow should never have fallen to the extent it did, given the readings their best computer guidance was providing them.

Bomb depressions on this scale only affect

OPPOSITE: A rare sight — snow to sea level puts the Canterbury coastline in sharp detail in this image captured by the MODIS Terra satellite the day after the big storm.

New Zealand once every few years. However, all that's on average; there could be more in 2006 and then none for a decade. All it takes is a subtle change of tack for the next one to affect Marlborough or Otago rather than Canterbury. This system barely registered on weather maps on Saturday 10 June, but had become a fearsome, mid-latitude storm 24 hours later.

The vigorous mixing of different air masses was a major factor behind the system's explosive deepening. Ahead of the depression were warm and moist north-westerly winds, while cold southerlies were chasing along in its wake. What turned this from a typical Tasman Sea depression into a meteorological maverick was its position, wedged between two jet streams.

These ribbons of strong winds at high altitude act like high-speed vacuum cleaners. If a surface system is located in the right position underneath one, it will effectively suck air from the top of the depression and speed up the rate at which it is spinning, increasing the upward motion that forms cloud, rain and snow, and further lowering air pressure at the surface.

Bomb lows of this kind are far more common in the North Atlantic Ocean, where air masses with huge temperature contrasts do battle and fuel violent systems that can cause major damage and huge swells. On the less frequent occasions when our weather forecasters have to confront these renegades, New Zealand's rugged terrain makes them even more difficult to deal with.

The Southern Alps have a huge influence on our weather in all kinds of ways, lying almost at right angles and acting as a barrier to weather systems that generally move from west to east. A deepening depression approaching the South Island will not simply move across the island as one system. Instead, the low air pressure is effectively transferred from one side of the island to the other. New depression centres form to the east of the ranges as the original cores of low pressure weaken west of the Main Divide.

Forecasters need to know very accurately where those new centres will form to be able to predict the location of the worst weather. That was the case in this storm, with very cold air from the south-west arriving over the region at the same time as a low pressure vortex wound up off the North Canterbury coast. It was only when this whirligig moved further offshore in the afternoon that the snow stopped falling.

FORECASTING THE FUTURE

Many lessons will be learnt from the storm, but there may be little that weather forecasters can glean from events to enable them to issue more accurate predictions next time. Despite their expertise, their observing network and the multi-million dollar technology at their finger tips, they say they may never be able to precisely predict these bombs and where they will hit hardest. Cantabrians, particularly those whose safety and livelihood depend on the weather, would be advised to keep watching the sky and checking their barometers.

There will be another bomb. It could be this year, next year or in 20 years. This time it came before lambing and moved away quite quickly; next time it may stall over Canterbury and bring even more snow. Nobody can doubt the June 2006 event has earned its place in the snow storm rogues' gallery, along with the storms of August 1992, August 1973, November 1967 and July 1945.

Paul Gorman and John Keast

OPPOSITE: Colder out than in — a staff member watches over the Hanmer Springs hot pools.

Passengers wait for weather to clear at Christchurch Airport after many flights were cancelled because of the foul weather.

The Waimakariri River, swollen by heavy rain and snow, surges under the State Highway 1 motorway bridge just north of Christchurch.

Lots of snow and no school: Sam Thomas carries his sled up Hackthorne Road in the Christchurch hill suburb of Cashmere.

A tough day to be a taxi driver: Ida McNicholl, left, Joseph Yang and Igor Boufal wait for fares at Christchurch Airport despite many flight cancellations.

Hagley Park on a snowy morning.

In this much snow, it is safer to walk: Cranmer Square, central Christchurch.

Hugh Taylor moving electric fences on his View Hill farm.

The statue of Queen Victoria stands stoically over the dusting of snow in Victoria Square, central Christchurch.

A fallen tree lies across power wires and the midland rail line near Darfield.

Road maintenance contractor Fulton Hogan was busy throughout the region. Here a truck clears snow from State Highway 73 in Darfield.

Ross Jackson, owner of the Rakaia River Holiday Park, wonders where to begin.

John Clyne of Waddington clears snow from his car after getting stuck in Ritso Street, Darfield.

Inland towns like Geraldine experienced some of the heaviest falls.

Kyle Campbell of Rakaia braves the snow to buy some beer.

A bleak morning for a flock of sheep at Rakaia.

Kaiapoi-based logging trucks lead a convoy across the Rakaia River after the road opening mid-morning.

ABOVE: At 11.30 am, Gail Williams, a traffic manager for Fulton Hogan, was still at her post on the outskirts of Springfield after starting her shift at 3 am.

LEFT: A stranded truck gets a tow on State Highway 1 just north of the Rakaia River.

State Highway 1 just south of Rolleston was reduced to one slow lane.

Kevin Matkin had to shovel the snow away from his car on Wai-iti Road, Timaru, before he could get to work.

The rare sight of Timaru lying under snow down to sea level.

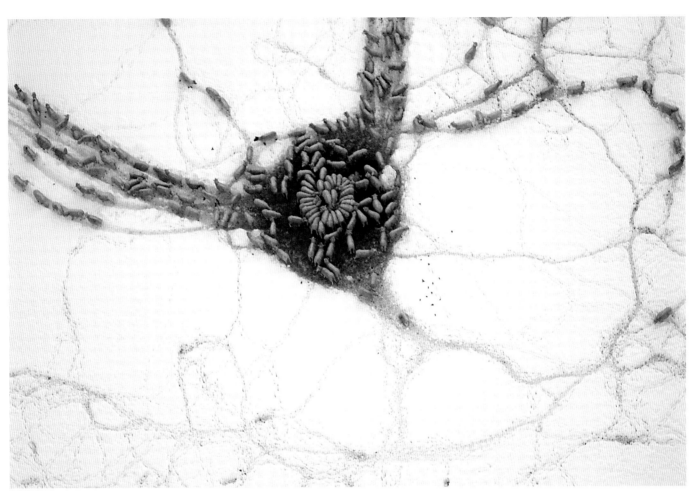

An aerial shot of sheep being fed out in the snow near Geraldine.

There's nothing like an ice-cold beer: the DB brewery, Timaru.

The Fairlie basin, with the township in the middle distance, was among the hardest hit, in terms of depth of snow and the time taken to restore vital services.

ABOVE: Power lines downed by the weight of snow on a side road near Waddington.

OPPOSITE TOP: Mt Hutt skifield, looking back towards Christchurch. The field had already enjoyed an early opening for the season, but was set up for a bumper winter with a further 85 cm of snow from the storm.

OPPOSITE BOTTOM: Kerry McTavish, riding Roc-it, tows snowboarding husband Rory across a Waikuku paddock, with Oska chasing behind.

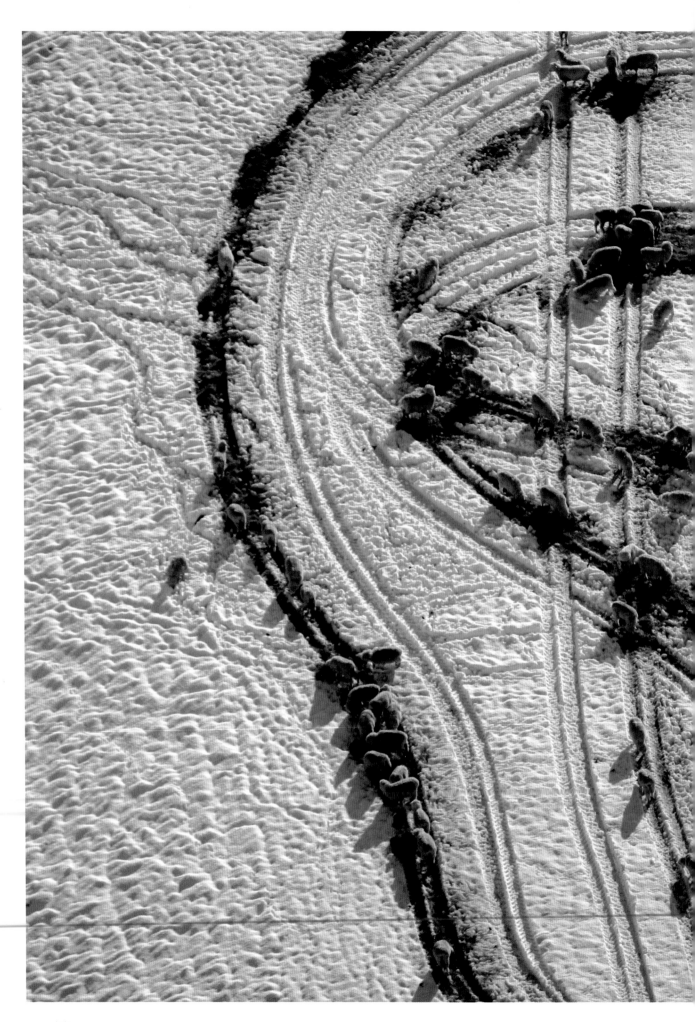

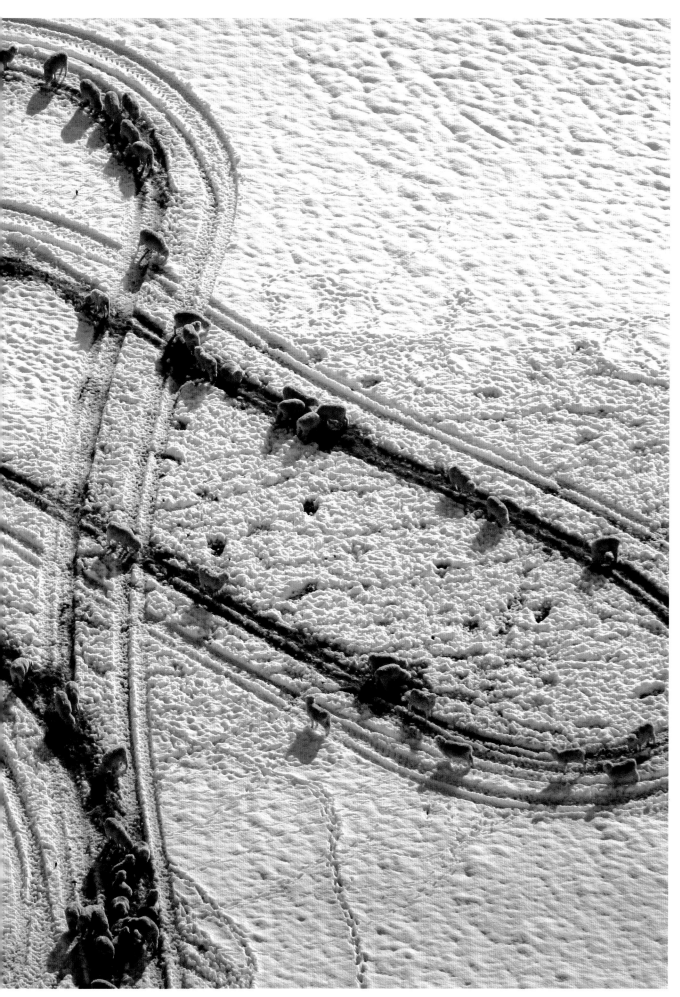

Grateful sheep gather along a line of feed curled through their paddock in South Canterbury.

ABOVE: The port of Timaru with snow to sea level.

OPPOSITE TOP: Snow train to nowhere — a coal train stands on the midland line, halted by fallen trees and power lines across the tracks between Waddington and Darfield.

OPPOSITE CENTRE: A grader clears snow from the runway at the Richard Pearse Airport, Timaru.

OPPOSITE BOTTOM: Snow mayhem in central Geraldine.

Timaru mayor Janie Annear in Geraldine, where council staff used portable radios while telephone services were affected by power cuts.

A good samaritan clears the walkways in the main street of Fairlie in the isolated Central South Island, which had been snow bound for five days.

Headstones in a cemetery at the intersection of Buchanans Road and State Highway 73 on the outskirts of Christchurch.

ABOVE: Geraldine residents Evelyn and Rick Pitelen, left, get help clearing their drive from Jadin Leonard and his dad Rodger.

OPPOSITE TOP: Doug Sanders and daughter Sophie, 11, seen riding their special track-adapted quad bike, got through the power cuts on their Geraldine farmlet with candles and a fire with a wetback.

OPPOSITE BOTTOM: Sherri Blair and Brian Mowat-Gainsford try out an Argo all-terrain vehicle on Peel Street, Geraldine.

Barbara Reid on a delivery trip with hot food for her daughter in Geraldine.

Dawn Gresham survived the cold and power cuts in her century-old cottage in Geraldine by taking the front off her logburner so she could slide a pot inside for cooking.

Snow-swathed Geraldine sparkles in the sun.

Thick snow blankets the Fairlie basin, looking south.

Farmland near Christchurch, looking across the south-west suburbs to the Port Hills.

Cleared of snow, the West Coast Road stands out in this view of Darfield looking back towards Christchurch.

The snow appears relatively light in the Yaldhurst area, on the south-west outskirts of Christchurch.

The town of Ashburton, with the Recreation Reserve, centre.

Shannon Quinn, Heather Crawford, Sharni Killoran and Nicole Latimer having fun in the snow at Geraldine.

No weather for swimming: Timaru with the Century Indoor Pool in the foreground.

Low sun adds a rose tint to the township of Pareora, about 10 km south of Timaru.

Lake Pukaki in the snow.

Searching for food at View Hill, near Oxford. The Torlesse Range is in the background.

ABOVE: Hugh Taylor moves cattle in search of feed on his farm at View Hill, near Oxford in North Canterbury.

OPPOSITE: Laurie Squires, who survived without power with the help of a gas barbecue, at her home near Hororata.

The Tekapo canal, in the Mackenzie Basin, continued its vital work of feeding water to the upper Waitaki power scheme while national power usage figures hit new highs.

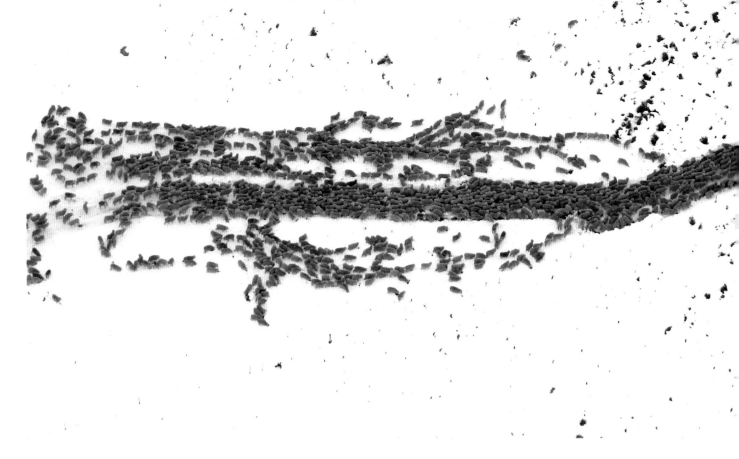

Sheep gather in search of rare feed in the snow-covered tussock of the Mackenzie.

Privates Anita Winders, left, Andrew Younson, and Keenan Williams of 3 Transport Platoon at Burnham Military Camp prepare to load up with the help of Lance Corporal Chris Rae (rear, in the Unimog) to go to the assistance of the snow-bound residents of Canterbury.

Heavy cost: a rental cottage owned by Robert Braham and his wife, Sue, near Mt Somers was lost to fire because they first had to drive to raise the alarm because of the telephone outage, then the Fire Brigade was delayed in arrival by the snow-bound roads.

Be prepared: Samantha Doak, 4, helps her family stock up on batteries in the New World supermarket, Ashburton.

Waimakariri River in flood under the State Highway 1 motorway bridge after heavy rain and snow fell over night.

Neryl Chapman walks her dog Dougal past the piles of snow cleared from the main street in Fairlie.

A team of snow-rakers, who rescue snow stranded stock, prepare to leave by helicopter from Fairlie.

Making plans for hay delivery: Mackenzie farmer Victoria Simpson with Fairlie Civil Defence Officer Leo Crampton, right, and Burnham soldiers Lance Corporal Lisa Avery, left, and Corporal Don Killgrove on the Simpson family farm at Mt Nessing.

A loader and truck work to clear the main street of Fairlie five days after the big fall.

Close call: no-one was hurt when this Hughes 500 helicopter crashed in the snow while doing a wire check on the isolated Lochaber Station, inland from Fairlie.

ABOVE: A snow plough and grit spreader leads a small convoy through Porters Pass.

RIGHT: Sheep in the snow near Springfield.

Snowboarders get a tow from a car on Church Street, Timaru.

Contractors Paul Burnaby, left, and Anthony Mohi, who came from the North Island to help restore the battered power system, work on an 11 kV line at Lowcliffe, near the Rangitata River mouth, which had been out for 12 days.

OPPOSITE: A tractor on Porters Pass.

ABOVE: A young calf faces more fresh snow on a paddock near Methven.

OPPOSITE TOP: Loving life! Feeling right at home in the Ashburton Domain are George, a husky, front, and Hannibal, an Alaskan malamute.

OPPOSITE BOTTOM: Grey skies herald another fall of snow on a paddock near Methven.

National Library of New Zealand Cataloguing-in-Publication
Data available on request

A RANDOM HOUSE BOOK
published by
Random House New Zealand
18 Poland Road, Glenfield, Auckland, New Zealand
www.randomhouse.co.nz

First published 2006, reprinted 2006

The NIWA graphic on p. 5 was reproduced from Hendrikx, J.,
2006. Preliminary analysis of the 12 June 2006 Canterbury
snow storm. NIWA Client Report, CHC2006-088, prepared
for Orion New Zealand Ltd., 26 pp (available from www.
niwascience.co.nz/pubs/mr/archive/2006-07-04-1/).

ISBN 1 86941 871 9
ISBN 978 1 86941 871 7

Cover and text design by Katy Yiakmis
Printed in Christchurch by Wyatt & Wilson Print Ltd

PHOTOGRAPH CREDITS

Carys Monteath: p. 14 bottom, p. 30 bottom
David Alexander: front cover bottom right, p. 15 top and
bottom, p. 18 top, p. 23, p. 31, p. 34 top and bottom,
p. 36, p. 37 bottom, p. 38, p. 39 top and bottom, p. 40,
p. 41 top and bottom, p. 50
David Hallett: p. 9, pp. 58–59 top and bottom, p. 61
Dean Kozanic: p. 2, p.12 bottom, p.13
Don Scott: front cover bottom left, p. 3, pp. 16–17, p. 19, pp.
20–21, p. 22 top and bottom, pp. 24–25, pp. 28–29, p. 30
top, pp. 32–33, p. 34 middle, pp. 34–35 right, pp. 42–43,
p. 44 top and bottom, p. 45 top and bottom
John Bisset (*The Timaru Herald*): front cover top, p. 1,
p. 18 bottom, p. 26 top and bottom, p. 27 top and bottom,
p. 46, p. 47 top and bottom, p. 48, p. 52, p. 53 top, p. 60
top, p. 64, back cover
John Keast: p. 57 bottom right
John Kirk-Anderson: front cover bottom middle, p. 14 top,
p. 49, p. 51
Kirk Hargreaves: p. 54 top, p. 55 top, p. 62 top and bottom,
p. 63
Peter Meecham: p.10 top, p.11, p.12 top, p. 37 top, pp. 56–
57 top, p. 56 bottom left and bottom right, p. 57 bottom
left
Stacy Squires: p.10 bottom, p. 53 bottom, pp. 54–55
bottom, p. 60 bottom

The moon rises over snow-clad South Canterbury.